STILL RHYMIN'
ON THE RANGE

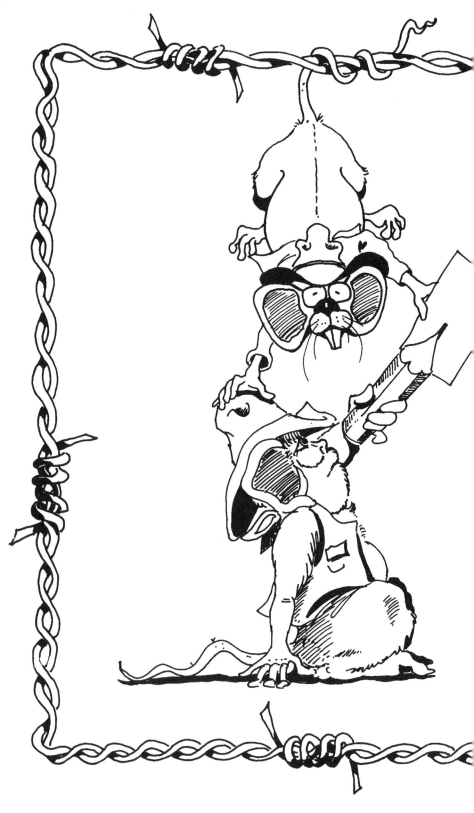

STILL RHYMIN' ON THE RANGE

Mike Puhallo Wendy Liddle Brian Brannon

hancock house

ISBN 0-88839-388-1
Copyright © 1996 Mike Puhallo, Brian Brannon, Wendy Liddle

Cataloging in Publication Data
Puhallo, Mike, 1953-
   Still rhymin' on the range
   ISBN 0-88839-388-1

   1. Cowboys—Poetry. 2. Cowboys' writings, Canadian (Eng-
lish)—British Columbia.* 3. Canadian poetry (English)—British
Columbia.* 4. Canadian poetry (English)—20th century.* I. Bran-
non, Brian, 1946- II. Title.
   PS8581.U42S8 1996   C811'.5408'0352636   C96-910029-9
   PR9199.3.P85S8 1996

Production: Nancy Miller and Myron Shutty
Editing: Nancy Miller
Cover: Mike Puhallo

Published simultaneously in Canada and the United States by

HANCOCK HOUSE PUBLISHERS LTD.
19313 Zero Avenue, Surrey, B.C. V4P 1M7
(604) 538-1114 Fax (604) 538-2262

HANCOCK HOUSE PUBLISHERS
1431 Harrison Avenue, Blaine, WA 98230-5005
(604) 538-1114 Fax (604) 538-2262

Contents

Acknowledgments

First, a thank you to those who read our first book, *Rhymes on the Range*, without your support we couldn't have put this volume out. We must also thank Hancock House for taking a chance on three lunatic cow persons...twice!

We dedicate this book to Jeanette, Linda and Mark, and anyone else with a sense of humor and an appreciation of our western heritage.

P.S. The West ain't dead yet, as long as there's one cow left, there will be a cowboy somewhere lookin' for it!

Freedom

Mike Puhallo

Freedom is a blaze-faced bay,
long legs and lots of wind,
High meadows on the first of May
when the snow's finally thinned.

Moving water everywhere o'er the slippery rocks,
through one big sponge of grass and moss
that'll soak a hiker's socks.

But I pass by, snug and dry.
I ride a tall bay hoss.

Home from the Mountain

Mike Puhallo

There's a stillness and peace
that I can't explain
as I gaze at the beauty
of winter's domain.

From the peaks of the mountains
to the river below,
all nature seems dormant,
her shroud made of snow.

At the edge of the field,
near the haystack,
a lone pony stands, humped,
with snow on his back.

Across the field
there's a streamer of smoke.
From cabin to woodshed,
a fresh trail's been broke.

For a week on the trail,
I've cursed winter each day.
But now I'm damn near home;
what a beautiful day.

The Guide

Brian Brannon

There's a different kind of cowboy
    that you hardly ever see,
You won't find him in the movies
    or watch him on TV.

He don't wear no fancy Stetsons,
    no buckles made of gold;
His home is just a wall tent
    or he sleeps out in the cold.

If you meet him in the city,
    he might hardly say a thing.
But those who think him surly
    should meet him where he's king.

You've got to go up riding
    where it's high and wild and green
To see his long, ole' pack string
    cross an icy mountain stream.

Then...he'll tip his old Resistol
    and pass the time of day
With his leg hooked o'er the pommel
    till he moves along his way.

Because high up and lonesome
    is where he lives to be.
High up and lonesome
    with the eagles, 'bove the trees;
High up and lonesome
    you can see...
    and see...
    and see.

Advice

Mike Puhallo

Just scoot down in your saddle
and screw your hat down tight.
Any job is easier
if you hold your mouth just right!

They told me: turn your toes out,
watch his head, and lift your rein.
Arch your back and nod your noodle,
now spur him in the mane.

Was too much to remember
for a simple young cowhand.
Besides you can't see your toes
with your head stuck in the sand.

Well, as time went on I rode a few
and seemed to learn a bit.
But as for all that good advice,
it just didn't always fit.

I learned to ride the rank ones
and it seemed easy for a while,
till father time sneaked up on me
and sort of cramped my style.

My advice to you young twisters
who crave to ride them broncs,
is to dodge those barrel racers,
and stay out of honky tonks.

And when you're gettin' ready,
remember what I said.
Blow the B.S. out your ears
and try to clear your head.

All you really need to do is
screw your hat down tight,
scoot down in that saddle,
and hold your mouth just right!

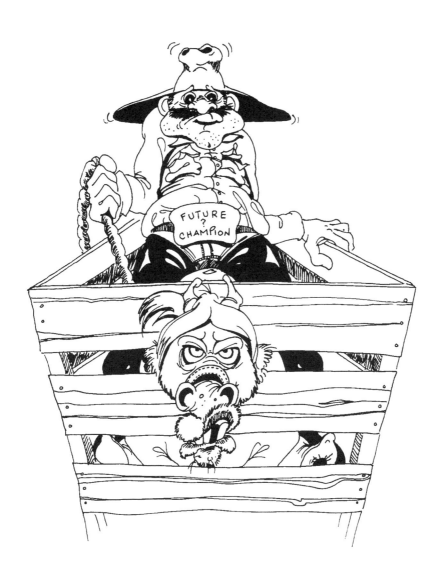

New to the North

Brian Brannon

Old Dave and I were ridin'
    a Yukon trail one night,
The trail was bathed in moonlight
    —the stars were shinin' bright.

Old Dave was up on Captain,
    that gray thought he was a stud.
I rode our mighty black horse,
    a trusted friend named Bud.

We were headed for the Rocking Star,
    a ranch Ostachek owns,
It lies at the head of Kluane Lake,
    the outfit calls it home.

We'd left moose camp on Grayling Creek
    some eighty miles ago.
For those that's never done the like,
    that's four sleeps in the snow.

Each led a four-horse pack string
    all tied from tail to head.
And for that trail we rode upon
    I'd have none in their stead.

There was Pepper, Gem and Bogart,
    this moose-cross called Banjo,
Young Junior, Blaze and Laddie,
    and another black named Beau.

T'was half-an-hour past midnight,
    or somewheres there about,
For we'd been pushin' plenty hard;
    our ponies short on oats.

We were reachin' for the Little Arm,
   there's a sheep-camp cabin there.
"We'll find some grub for horse and man,"
   old Davie did declare.

Then came this eerie, moanin' sound,
   I swear it filled the night.
I thought it must be grizzly bear
   or moose cow filled with fright.

So I calls up the line to Davie-boy,
   a peerless old bush rat,
"You've rode these mountains many years,
   just what in hell is that?

"I figure it might be a demon from Hades
   or a banshee from Ireland's shores.
I've rode in the hills a few years, too,
   but I've not heard its like before."

Well, old Davie he started in laughin',
   his cacklin' it filled the night air.
I figured my pardner had come unglued,
   he'd fall off his pony for fair.

When Dave finally got himself back together,
   that worthy he yells back to me,
"You drippy-eared, face-fuzzy greenhorn,
   you're damned sure a pilgrim I see.

"That's neither a ghost, nor a goblin;
   no demon, nor banshee to fear.
You'd best dab a loop on your Irish,
   that's a freezin' up river you hear.

"And son let me tell you another,
   if you think when she's freezin' it's loud
You should hear the din in the springtime
   when the ice blocks come down in a crowd!"

Well, we pulled in the gates of the Rockin' Star
    that very next day like we planned.
Drew our bonuses, wages, and left with the boys,
    went to Whitehorse, got drunk to the man.

And it's been quite a while since I left there
    but I'll never forget, don't ya know,
That sound in the night of the ice freezin' up
    as two cowboys rode by in the snow.

Bugs

Mike Puhallo

Of all the critters on this earth,
    I think BUGS have got it BEST!
no fussin' 'bout the mortgage,
    with a cowpie for a nest.

Ze Best Cook of Ze Vildness

Brian Brannon

We work with German folks each year,
    we've come to plumb adore them.
We haul them over hill and dale
    on horses that deplore them.

There's some who'll speak English,
    and some that don't;
There's some who'll try to
    and lots that won't.

But when you put all that aside
    they can be plumb amusin'.
There's things they say that make my day
    my funny bone abusin'.

'Cause though we try our tongues to ply
    these different words and meanings,
We never seem to crack the code,
    can't break our national leanings.

Well, words are words, we live in herds
    and folks are folks no matter.
A man who loves a horse can't be
    from Satan's *alma mater*.

So grab your dictionaries friends
    we'll stumble on our way.
Someday we'll maybe break the wall,
    that's what this cowboy says.

Un Control

Mike Puhallo

We've got a brand new edict,
    from them jerks in Ottawa,
to own an unlicensed firearm,
    is now against the law!

So I buried my grandfather's pistol
    out in the alfalfa field,
Wrapped in layers of well-oiled rags
    and a tupperware box it is sealed.

I don't know if the damn thing shoots anymore;
    it is at least a hundred years old,
but it's part of grandfather's legacy,
    more precious to me than gold.

When he was young, grandpa carried that piece
    ridin' the Alberta plains,
and passed it to my father
    when he cowboyed the Chilcotin range.

That ol' Smith revolver and a Winchester '94
    was all that grandfather left me
when he passed heaven's door.
    Now three generations of stockmen
have carried them guns on this land
    and they've never spoken in anger,
'though perhaps the time is at hand.

Ice and Stone

Brian Brannon

I took this scientific guy
    out in the hills one time,
And for another trip like that
    I wouldn't give a dime.

For though the land we rode upon
    was shamin' paradise,
This yokel never cared about
    a thing but rock and ice.

The weather, it was gorgeous.
    The sun it shone each day.
I showed him God's creative best
    as I tried to earn my pay.

But whether it was mountains
    or valleys 'bound with game,
This mother lover's firm demand
    was every day the same.

Glaciers, glaciers, ice and stone,
    that's all he cared to see.
I really couldn't fathom it,
    that all seems dead to me.

Oh yeah, I know they've shaped the earth,
    they've given the land its form.
But his obsessive interest
    seemed way beyond the norm.

And so at night, 'round campfire bright,
    I tried to understand
Through talk and jest, comradery,
    what drove that haunted man.

But though I talked till I was blue,
    I couldn't crack his shell.
And so the trip, from one night forth
    was like a ride through hell.

No smiles were seen, our meals were lean
    the horses couldn't handle
That frozen, lifeless, hint of man,
    oh boys, go light a candle.

T'was one and twenty days, me lads,
    till Tuscha showed her shores.
We thanked the gods of horse and man
    to shed what we abhorred.

I swore that day I never would
    go forth with one alone,
Especially if he loved the sight
    of glacier, ice and stone.

Dylan's Candle

Mike Puhallo

My candle burns upon both ends,
It will not last the night,
But shining for all to see,
It makes a lovely light.
      —Dylan Thomas

I'm burning Dylan's candle,
and the Welshman didn't lie.
There's a force that drives a poet,
that he simply can't deny.

Forgotten words and passions,
tumble from my pen.
Welling somewhere from within,
I know not how or when!

Sleep is driven from my thoughts,
when the urge is on to write
unaware of time or place,
I scribble on through the night.

Sweet memories and dreams
dance across my page;
Of carefree youth
spent in those hills of bunchgrass, pine and sage.

I write though I'm exhausted,
if I try to stand, I fall.
Enslaved by the pen, till the tale will end,
I'm immune to *Morpheus'* call.

The Guide's Dilemma

Brian Brannon

Have you ever walked a glacier
    with a sheep head on your back,
Have you felt the ice a-groanin,
    have you seen those yawning cracks?

Have you heard the ravens crying
    in the rocks above your head?
Have you mourned that wondrous creature
    that your hunter's just left dead?

Have you trudged those seeming hours
    to the horses tied below?
Have you felt that cold wind blowin',
    have you watched that sunset's glow?

Do you call yourself a hunter
    while you think yourself a fool?
Are you kin to old Jim Bridger
    or are you just a tool?

Do you feel it's somehow worth it
    'cause you love to ride a horse?
Is it part of man's perversion
    or part of nature's course?

My Place

Brian Brannon

High up
    above the timberline,
On windswept peaks
    of crumbling stone,
The sky
    in sunlight
Is palest blue.
    And goat trails are sensed,
Rather than seen.

Fast

Mike Puhallo

Calavaras County may have its jumping frogs,
    and there's tracks around the country
where they race with nags or dogs.
    And I've seen those big ol' Brahma bulls
put brave young men to flight.
    But none move like my brother
when his bride gets on the fight!

The Bear

Brian Brannon

There's folks that'll yap about grizzlies,
    they'll tell you they know what they say.
They'll tell you, that bear, he's a killer.
    He's vicious near every way.

You may ask what's different 'bout me,
    you might say you've heard it before,
But I've spent many years in his mountains...
    I know him right down to the core.

And pards, let me tell you, I've been close
    when he didn't know I was there.
He's far from the monster they make him,
    he's just hisself bein' a bear.

That bear he likes fun, he's got courage,
    he lives to the full every day.
He knows how to mind his own business,
    which is more than most humans can say.

I reckon that's why there'll always be trouble
    'twixt man and the grizzly bear clan.
Respect is a thing we should learn well
    before we trespass on his land.

Yeah, you read me damned right, I'm on his side
    and I can't but believe that I'm right.
Before I'll see mountains without him,
    I'll just have to join in the fight.

Old Blue

Brian Brannon

When I met Old Blue he was gettin' on,
    twenty-five winters he'd seen.
A blue-black roan with jewel-like eyes,
    he stood sixteen hands and lean.

He bore a great scar 'round the base of his neck,
    like the corded roots of a tree.
And though none could say where he got it
    t'was the mark of a snare to me.

You know the meat hunters prey on wild horse herds
    and it's sometimes they use 'em a snare.
They'll get 'em their pounds and their dollars
    with neither a thought nor a care.

Old Blue, he's a point in my story,
    a horse like him rarely is seen.
I'm sure that he ran with the wild bunch,
    yet a greater horse hasn't been.

He'd take Man O'War to his paces,
    and serve as a pack horse as well.
There's very few things that he can't do
    I'm here as his witness to tell.

So friends, bear his story in mind,
    never judge by its cover, a book.
There's horse out there that'll fool you,
    we owe them that extra look.

Water Wagon

Mike Puhallo

There was a rodeo at Gottfriedson's
when I was just a lad.
I asked old Gus about my draw.
He said, "She ain't that bad."

Her name was Water Wagon
which sure seemed strange to me.
When I asked old Gus about that name,
he just smiled and said, "You'll see!"

I measured up my bronc rein
and climbed aboard the bay.
When the gate flew open,
she began to buck and spray!

To say the least it was distractin'
and didn't smell that good.
So, I didn't really lift and charge
the way a cowboy should.

Now, I've been bucked off lots of times
so that part didn't hurt.
At least not as much as what happened next
as I lay there in the dirt.

"Did you figure that name out yet?"
I heard Gus shout with glee
as old Water Wagon rolled on by
and peed all over me!

Requiem for NR

Brian Brannon

When I met NR at Bakers' Creek
    we was both in Brewsters' pay.
I was pullin' down eleven and found,
    NR was gettin' oats and hay.

He was lyin' up there in a porta-corral
    at the heard of the Baker Creek trail.
And the stud hand said, "Try to get him to work,
    everything we've tried has failed."

It's a heartbreak to put shoes on his feet,
    he's tossed all the summer hands.
I'll give you a season to bring him around,
    if you can't he goes in a can.

Well, a horseman won't see a savable horse
    go down in a meat buyer's book.
So I walked on over, leaned my arms on the rails
    and had me a closer look.

What I saw in there was covered in mud
    like a monarch bull in the rut.
And the gleam in its eye said, "I'll have my way
    no ifs, no ands, no buts."

He stood sixteen hands in four white socks
    and he filled out a massive frame.
He had an NR Bar on his onside hip,
    guess that's how the bay got his name.

And it was a tussle gettin' boots on his feet
    but he taught himself the way.
And we went through a time he tried to put me off
    nearly each and every day.

But he came around to be a damned fine horse
    he'd pull a six-horse string up a hill.
Though I worked him to death all season long,
    he never seemed to get his fill.

When the aspen leaves turned a shade of gold
    the boss tried to sell him to me.
But as cowboys will, I'd let my cash slip away,
    I had no money you see.

Well, as time went by, I kept an eye on NR
    Kevin sold him to a buckin' string.
I talked to Doug Richards at a rodeo,
    he said that horse wouldn't do a thing.

He was outlaw enough when he wanted to be,
    but he wasn't no rodeo fan.
The truth of my tale has a sad endin'
    NR ended up in a can.

Cowboy Arteest

Mike Puhallo

When this middle-aged cow puncher
    set out to learn to paint
they said, "If you're lookin' for a prosperous trade,
    this art stuff really ain't."
Well, thank you for that good advice,
    and I respect your point of view.
But, they say an artist has to starve,
    and if what they say is true,
Hell, I bin raisin' cows all my life,
    so it won't be nothing new!

Borrowed Horses

Mike Puhallo

The whole thing was Ted Vayros' fault.
I wanna make that plain.
Him and that bald-faced stud of his
can't dodge their share of blame.

      With cows to move and salt to pack
      and cuttin' a trail our goal,
      We run plum out of horses
      'cause our mares were all in foal.

Now the panniers are smashed to hell,
and the chainsaw's in the crick.
My shoulder's sore and my boots are wet,
and them skeeters sure are thick.

      They said the bay had packed before,
      but you can't prove that by me.
      And the pinto I borrowed from old Joe
      was green as he could be.

Now I'm trackin' that pair of runaways
through the swamps and mud.
And I'm cussin' borrowed horses
and Ted's old bald-faced stud!

Goofy

Brian Brannon

Goofy's a horse that I ride at Yohetta,
  a bay with some thoroughbred leanin's.
He makes it his business to live to his name,
  I figure you will catch my meanin'.

He'll look in the face of a thirty-yard grizzly
  and raise not a hackle nor hair.
But the dart of a squirrel or a grouse on the trailside
  can cause him to dance on the air.

And he'll try you sometimes in the mist of the mornin'
  just to see if your hat's screwed on tight.
Tell me, dear friends, how he knows near for certain
  we'd a goin' away party the previous night.

Well, as friends do, I probably harp on his bad side
  but ya'all know that ain't half the truth.
If I put my mind down to listin' his good points
  I could probably burn up my youth.

Like the fact that he'll power from can see to can't see
  and the mountains don't mean a damned thing.
I can let him graze loose on the grass of Long Meadow
  while some purebloods get tied to a string.

Don't he know all the trails, can't he see in the dark,
  ain't there a map to each camp in his head?
Don't he get only oats at the end of each day
  while I reap the brown points in his stead?

I really can't say who's a horseman,
  a breeder, a trainer, a seer.
Do Dorrance or Braynard or Hunt have the answers?
  That question will long hang, I fear.

I only know that we fit well together,
   a well-oiled hand in a glove.
Some people might say that I've trained him to pieces
   but we know he does it from love.

So what if he is just a little bit goofy,
   and he fits just a bit on the rim?
That really don't matter a whole lot to me folks,
   'cause I'm a whole lot like him.

One Shot McLean

Mike Puhallo

I rode with him in '70
He was seventy-six years old.
I was a boy of seventeen,
and Lord, what tales he told!
He was a legend on the Bonaparte
and up on Deadman Creek,
A quiet old man who lived alone;
But wasn't exactly meek.

He'd seen this land through an Indian's eyes,
when it was wild and free
and, because I'd sit and listen,
such stories he told me.
Some truth, some lies, some legend
and some just plain B.S.
The way good stories should be told,
the way I'll pass them on, I guess.

The last of the "Wild McLeans"
he taught me to love the wild;
in those high and rocky places,
when I was still a child.

Wondering Where the Lions Are

Mike Puhallo

Our politicians might improve
    if we tried the Roman way.
'Cause there's too many lies
    and not enough lions
in the arena of today.

Apostle of the Pack String

Brian Brannon

Now, cowboys they talk of Casey Tibbs
    of Russell, and old Will James.
Wherever there's a brandin' fire
    you'll hear those mighty names.

There's Goodnight,
    Loving, Chisholm, too,
and now Tom Blasingame.
    Hell, if the truth be known,
Tom Dorrance is gatherin' fame.

Young Casey, he was a ridin' fool
    of twistin' broncs supreme.
And Goodnight brought his Longhorns up
    while others just sat and dreamed.

Will James, he wrote those wondrous tales,
    inspired us all it seems.
And Charlie, he painted those priceless works
    with nickels and dimes in his jeans.

Now boys, for sure there is no doubt
    these gents have earned their names.
But friends, a good man's missing from
    this campfire hall of fame.

From Dubois, down Wyoming way,
    a packin' legend came.
And pards, he'd figure me plumb loco
    if he heard me make that claim.

For boys, Joe Back was a humble man
    with the average packer's hope.
Just to spend his life in a love affair
    with the high-up, windy slopes.

But like those we've named, Joe rose above
    the average packin' dope.
'Cause he knew the ways like a master, born
    of the diamond hitchin' ropes.

So boys recall, if you ride at all
    'mongst the high up lonesome hills,
Joe's the packin' best, he belongs with the rest
    his Whites will be hard to fill.

Deb Copenhaver's Cafe

Mike Puhallo

There's a salty old bronc rider
    that lives down Creston way.
He runs a little road house
    the boys call Deb's Cafe.

There's a dance hall out the back,
    where I've sipped a beer or two,
in the company of Ol' Deb himself,
    when we talked the whole night through.

We've talked about the old hands,
    some retired and some passed on.
And old Deb's got a million stories
    to pass the time till dawn.

Well every hand that passes by
    will stop along the way
for hot coffee and a burger
    down at Deb's Cafe.

But it ain't the food that draws them,
    it's those pictures on the wall.
A who's who of rodeo history
    'cause ol' Deb knew 'em all!

Bill Linderman has a special place;
    he was Deb's old travelin' pard.
And you know that when the King cashed in,
    he took it kind of hard!

There's Kenny McLean and Casey Tibbs,
    all the great ones of the day.
There's lots of cowboy history
    on the walls of Deb's Cafe.

If you're drivin' the state of Washington,
　　just west of Spokane,
in the little town of Creston
　　pull over if you can.

The coffee's hot and the grub is good,
　　the best along the way.
And you've got to see the pictures,
　　on the wall of Deb's Cafe!

Political Haze

Mike Puhallo

The sunshine of our rural life
is fading fast these days,
polluted from our cities
by a murky legal haze.

       You can't chase a cow, across the road
       unless you check the rules
       seems our governments and councils
       are stuffed right full of fools.

Each year in our great rivers
Tons of salmon die and rot.
But, let a cow poop on the river bank
and our city council's hot!

       They trip upon each other
       to show how "green" they are,
       and pass a law to save all trees
       no matter where they are.

Except the ones in urban lots,
five acres was the law.
Not many lots downtown that size,
and therein lies the flaw.

       Does this mean our ranch is now a park
       and I can cut no wood?
       I'd go and cuss the fools again
       But it would do no good.

They tell us where and how to live
from in their urban lair
and they ignore us country folk
when we say, "It just ain't fair!"

Us rural folk have lost again,
like sacrificial goats,
our rights and wishes
don't mean squat!
'cause town folk have more votes.

A Name Taking

Brian Brannon

I heard an old Nez Perce say,
    "Our people have forgotten
The ties that bound when Joseph lived
    are cast aside and broken.

"All who knew the earth have gone,
    our children do not listen.
Who will an old man teach the ways
    to honor plain and mountain?"

"Old One," said I, "I claim no right
    by blood to speak in council,
Yet I would have your spirit hear
    its death song sung unfretful.

"Great One," said I, "I share your love,
    this earth I, too, call mother.
So I would take your sacred trust
    and bear it as a brother.

"Grandfather, I know your heart,
    you fear that with your passing
No one will seek to know the earth,
    nor give no rites, no blessings.

"Go now Old One, you've earned your rest,
    your bones are old and creaking.
If you speak of me in the spirit world,
    may I be called Hears The Earth Speaking."

Family Tree

Mike Puhallo

Horsemen through the ages
have graced my family line
as far back as one can see
through the shifting sands of time.

Calvary men and teamsters,
on both my parents side.
Equestrians of every type
have been our family's pride.

They've herded sheep and cattle,
on the mountains and the plains,
and as time went by
each in turn has handed on the reins.

True, a few men from our family,
have worked at city trades.
But as a matter of consensus,
they's just renegades!

Through the life of ranch and rodeo,
the tradition's still alive.
And any time I have a choice,
I'd sooner ride then drive.

The point I'm trying to make,
and will before I quit,
is, if you're going to draw my family tree,
best tie a horse to it.

Children of the Soil

Mike Puhallo

As the cowboy rides the sagebrush hills,
the farmer tills the land.
The simple truths of nature,
    are theirs to understand.

The guide that rides the mountains,
and the trapper hunting fur,
know the earth does not belong to us,
    we belong to her.

A Clean Getaway

Sharlene Rose Puhallo

When I catch that rustler
    I'll give him no slack,
for I know which cow is missing,
    it's the old angus
with the stripe down her back.

Now there's muffins and apples
    left on the trail.
They're fresh as new hay
    wrapped in a bale.

I'm getting close, I can feel it now.
    By gum, there's the calf,
but where's the rustler and cow?

There's tire tracks goin' that way.
    I guess I'm too late, the rustler has left,
And I have no insurance for cattle theft!

I'll take the calf back home that's a fact,
    but when I catch that rustler next time,
it had better be in the act!

Glossary

Angus:	a breed of cow.
Bay:	color of a horse, brown with a black mane and tail.
Bonaparte:	Bonaparte Plateau, an area in B.C.
Braynard:	famous North American horse trainer.
Buck rein:	braided halter shank, used by bronc riders.
Chisholm:	legendary founder of cattle industry.
Dorrance:	famous North American horse trainer.
Goodnight:	legendary founder of cattle industry.
Hunt:	famous North American horse trainer.
James, Will:	cowboy artist and writer.
Lift and charge:	a term among bronc riders for lifting on the rein and spurring agressively.
Loving:	legendary founder of cattle industry.
McLean, One Shot:	Cliff McLean 1894-1993, nephew of famous outlaw gang hung in the 1880s.
Morpheus:	something that induces or prolongs sleep.
Muffins and apples:	meadow muffins and road apples, or cowpies and horseturds.
Offside:	right.
Onside:	left.
Panniers:	packboxes.
Pommel:	front of saddle.
Rank horses:	hard to ride or bad-tempered.
Resistol:	brandname cowboy hat.
Russell, Charles:	great cowboy artist.
Stetson:	brandname cowboy hat.

Tibbs, Casey: many times world saddlebronc champion, "won the world" first time in 1949 at nineteen years of age.

Wild McLeans: outlaw gang from early B.C. history.

Northern Biographies

Alaska Calls
Virginia Neely
ISBN 0-88839-970-7

Bootlegger's Lady
Sager & Frye
ISBN 0-88839-976-6

Bush Flying
Robert S. Grant
ISBN 0-88839-350-4

Crazy Cooks & Gold Miners
Joyce Yardley
ISBN 0-88839-294-X

Descent into Madness
Vernon Frolick
ISBN 0-88839-300-8

Fogswamp: Life with Swans
Turner & McVeigh
ISBN 0-88839-104-8

Gang Ranch: Real Story
Judy Alsager
ISBN 0-88839-275-3

Journal of a Country Lawyer
E. C. Burton
ISBN 0-88839-364-4

Lady Rancher
Gertrude Roger
ISBN 0-88839-099-8

My Heart Soars
Chief Dan George
ISBN 0-88839-231-1

My Spirit Soars
Chief Dan George
ISBN 0-88839-233-8

Nahanni
Dick Turner
ISBN 0-88839-028-9

Novice in the North
Bill Robinson
ISBN 0-88839-977-4

Ralph Edwards of Lonesome Lake
Ed Gould
ISBN 0-88839-100-5

Ruffles on my Longjohns
Isabel Edwards
ISBN 0-88839-102-1

Where Mountains Touch Heaven
Ena Kingsnorth Powell
ISBN 0-88839-365-2

Wings of the North
Dick Turner
ISBN 0-88839-060-2

Yukon Lady
Hugh McLean
ISBN 0-88839-186-2

Yukoners
Harry Gordon-Cooper
ISBN 0-88839-232-X

History

Barkerville
Lorraine Harris
ISBN 0-88839-152-8

B.C.'s Own Railroad
Lorraine Harris
ISBN 0-88839-125-0

Buckskin, Blades and Biscuits
Allen Kent Johnston
ISBN 0-88839-363-6

Cariboo Gold Rush Story
Donald Waite
ISBN 0-88839-202-8

The Craigmont Story
Murphy Shewchuk
ISBN 0-88839-980-4

Curse of Gold
Elizabeth Hawkins
ISBN 0-88839-281-8

Early History of Port Moody
Dorothea M. Norton
ISBN 0-88839-197-8

End of Custer
Dale T. Schoenberger
ISBN 0-88839-288-5

Fishing in B.C.
Forester & Forester
ISBN 0-919654-43-6

Fraser Canyon Highway
Lorraine Harris
ISBN 0-88839-182-X

Fraser Canyon Story
Donald E. Waite
ISBN 0-88839-204-4

Fraser Valley Story
Donald E. Waite
ISBN 0-88839-203-6

Gold Creeks & Ghost Towns
N. L. (Bill) Barlee
ISBN 0-88839-988-X

Gold! Gold!
Joseph Petralia
ISBN 0-88839-118-8

Living with Logs
Donovan Clemson
ISBN 0-919654-44-4

Lost Mines & Historic Treasures
N. L. (Bill) Barlee
ISBN 0-88839-992-8

The Mackenzie Yesterday
Alfred P. Aquilina
ISBN 0-88839-083-1

Pioneering Aviation of the West
Lloyd M. Bungey
ISBN 0-88839-271-0

Power Quest
Carol Batdorf
ISBN 0-88839-240-0

Spirit Quest
Carol Batdorf
ISBN 0-88839-210-9

Totem Poles of the NW
D. Allen
ISBN 0-919654-83-5

Vancouver Recalled
Derek Pethick
ISBN 0-919654-09-6

When Buffalo Ran
George Bird Grinnell
ISBN 0-88839-258-3

Yukon Gold
Jim and Susan Preyde
ISBN 0-88839-362-8

Other Hancock House Titles

Robert Service
51/2 X 81/2, 64 pp. SC
ISBN 0-88839-223-0

Robert Service
51/2 X 81/2, 64 pp. SC
ISBN 0-88839-224-9

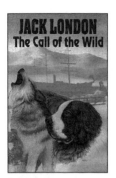

Jack London
51/2 X 81/2, 104 pp. SC
ISBN 0-88839-259-1

Chief Dan George and
Helmut Hirnschall
51/2 X 81/2, 96 pp. SC
ISBN 0-88839-231-1

Chief Dan George and
Helmut Hirnschall
51/2 X 81/2, 96 pp. SC
ISBN 0-88839-233-8

Mike Puhallo, Brian Brannon,
and Wendy Liddle
51/2 X 81/2, 64 pp. SC
ISBN 0-88839-368-7

Robert F. Harrington
51/2 X 81/2, 96 pp. SC
ISBN 0-88839-367-9

pj johnson
51/2 X 81/2, 64 pp. SC
ISBN 0-88839-366-0

James and Susan Preyde
51/2 X 81/2, 96 pp. SC
ISBN 0-88839-362-8

Available from Hancock House Publishers   19313 Zero Ave., Surrey, B.C. V4P 1M7
1-800-938-1114   Credit cards accepted.   1431 Harrison Ave., Blaine, WA 98230